Living Your Love Every Day

Volume One
Magical Moment

by
Judith Sherven and James Sniechowski

Dear Reader:

Perhaps you've only recently come to the work of psychologists Judith Sherven and Jim Sniechowski. Or maybe you're an old friend. In either case, please allow me to provide some background.

When Judith & Jim wrote this book - all 3 volumes - they lived in a charming old farmhouse in upstate New York and document much of their life there for us. What many people consider too painful or revealing to talk about, even with each other, this husband-and-wife team shares with us freely. What many couples run away from, these two face head on. That's why they entitled these volumes "Living Your Love Every Day."

Not only do Judith & Jim share their experiences, they also use them to show us examples we can use in our own relationships. In the smallest of disputes, the briefest intimate moments, we find new awareness. They have much to teach us.

Luckily, this three-volume set contains nearly a hundred short articles. Here, as in life, there's no set path you must follow. Savor one piece a day, read a dozen at a time, skip around, plough right through--it doesn't matter. Inside you'll find the best fun, daily romance, and other glimpses into Judith & Jim's marriage and their wisdom about real life love and romance.

Enjoy.

Yours Truly,
Signe A. Dayhoff, PhD

Author of "Attracting and Dating the Wrong Men? Tips and Insights to Free Yourself" on Kindle

Contents

Smooth seas do not make skillful sailors.
--African Proverb

1. INTIMACY—IT'S IN THE DIFFERENCES

This is a Book about love and intimacy. But where do you find love and intimacy

This may surprise you, but they are waiting in a place you probably haven't considered—in the differences between you and your partner, you and your date. The truth is, differences make up the heart and soul of long-term romance. They are the ground of individual discovery and mutual growth. They offer deep and abiding passion. To recognize, respect, and value the differences between you and someone you love will bring spiritual fulfillment achievable in no other way. When you open to the treasure of differences—a treasure right in front of you—there is a payoff. You'll realize what it's like to be loved for who you really are

This e-book is also about being who you are: your strengths and weaknesses, your ambitions and insecurities, your passions and prayers—it's about hiding nothing, about being eager, open, and willing to be known

But what about the other person? Your friend? Date? Lover? Mate? To create a successful and rewarding relationship you must be able to find value and significance in the different ways of others. When you do, and they reciprocate, you will know a grace and compassion that will support and sustain you for the challenges of real-life love

Many people shy away from intimacy—not just sexual intimacy but emotional and spiritual intimacy as well. Do you? Are you afraid that if someone really got to know you, he or she would...what? You probably have a list of what might happen. You would be rejected, laughed at, maybe even considered odd? Right? Are these on your list

Maybe. Yet if someone is serious about love and closeness, willing to be open, he or she will find in you someone eager to be loved and to give love in return. Someone—a real human being—who goes through ups and downs, someone with a heart and a history

It's too bad that so many people—men and women alike—are scared into hiding the very richest parts of themselves. We all do that. And then, because we know we are not being real, we struggle to find love. And if we're not being real, how can we trust anyone we're with

That's why for so many people love is never truly satisfying. People marry and don't feel loved (or loving). Dating? Just a joke. They feel lost in a desert, thirsting for something that may just be a mirage. Do you know what we mean

Do you want to be awake in your love and allow love to make you more fully alive? You have purchased and are

2

reading this e-book, so the answer must be yes

In the following pages we will explore many of the faces of intimacy and share with you its many possibilities—ways of making your relationships deeper, richer, sweeter and joyous. That's a promise!

Judith Sherven and James Sniechowski

Only between one person and another can the renewal of our world begin.
--John Welwood

2. TAKE THE CHANCE

We are now residents of Windham, NY. We moved here from Santa Monica, CA—to live in a 200-year-old farm house that sits on 2 acres and has its own pond

We are seeing how this move has opened us in so many ways—ways we could never have predicted. But first we had to trust our impulse

to take a big leap, to let go of a need for certainty. Of course, the same leap is required when any of us starts a new relationship or decides to give ourselves fully to a marriage that has been neglected

Here we are surrounded by more of God's beauty than we imagined. We live on a road dotted with old farm houses—some with horses, one with sheep in the front yard, another with pigs in the barn. The skies are a painter's dream. And we get to live here!! Why? Because we followed our yearning to move beyond a lifestyle that had become routine, to dance with life in a way that would challenge us to stay closer to the spirit of being fully alive, rather than clinging to the safe and predictable. We gave ourselves to the adventure of expanding intimacy—both with one another and with nature

Certainly this change has come with challenges: the water smelled of sulphur and left our skin slimy after a shower, mice visited the kitchen drawers and counters on a regular basis (it is an old farm house!), and the chimney was dangerously cracked. Little by little we are getting all these things taken care of

But if this were a romantic relationship, the love affair would most likely be over. Why? Because the reality would be too different from what is familiar. The need to grow into the challenges would not fit the expectations of love, it wouldn't be as it "should be.

Yet we are both much the richer for these encounters with reality. Each of us is more resilient, more flexible, more conscious of the positive blessings of our life here each and every day. We remark, almost daily, on the new joy we feel in being together, the deeper levels of intimacy

and tenderness we feel as a byproduct of going through these challenges side by side

Jim is learning how to put up wallpaper. Judith is learning to wear hiking boots and "farm" clothes. We're being changed in so many ways—and loving it

Our wish for you is that you release any old, outworn habits in your relationship(s) so that you can open up to more love in your life.

Choose one thing that you will do differently today. Let love play more in your life. Trust that it will be good for you. Even if you are scared or anxious, even if you feel

Judith Sherven and James Sniechowski

out of control—do it anyway!!!!

You must be the change
you wish to see in the world.
--Mahatma Gandhi

3. WE ALL NEED TO BE RECOGNIZED

Everyone wants to be recognized and valued—just **for being.** Sadly, many of us don't receive this kind of deep, solid validation of our worth from our parents. They didn't get it from their parents—who didn't get it from their parents, and so it goes. It's no one's fault, but it is a problem

Most people doubt their own value, doubt they will be well received when they meet new people, and even doubt the love of their spouse

Being new to this mountain community—Windham, New York—we are meeting lots of people for the first time. We'd been warned that, being new and obviously city folks, we would feel some prejudice and stand-offishness from some of the locals. So far that hasn't happened

.The people here have been very helpful and kind to us and we're even beginning to make new friends (who've invited us over for dinner—a genuine gourmet treat)

Nevertheless, Judith commented yesterday that, while her mind knows she is welcome and wanted here, her old

7

programming still rises up in fear once in a awhile—such as when we went into the local library to ask that they order our books for their stacks, or when she had to have the bank clerk help her figure out a new account. The old demons seem to lurk around, far more quietly than in the past, no matter how much work you do on yourself

So let's all remember that we can be more intimate, even with strangers. All it takes is an easy smile, a warm handshake, and a sincere "how's it goin'?" We can remember that everyone's feeling insecure in some way, and we understand. We've been there, too.

Make it a point to acknowledge all the people you encounter this weekend and notice how good it feels to spread intimacy in little ways.

It is in your relationship to the beloved that you come to your true nature.

--Kabir

4. MEDITATIONS ON A LITTLE RED FLOWER

The other day we took a walk out to a nearby field. Behind several tall pines, hidden away from open view, a single, small flower spread its blossoms toward the sun. It was a deep red, vivid—very strong and straight on its thin stem

"Proud," Jim said

"Proud and powerful," Judith answered

We both knelt next to it, captivated, surrendering to an unexpected meditation

So unseen this little red miracle was, so out of the way, and that didn't matter at all. Appreciated or not, it gave all it had to its life

"Can we give everything," Jim whispered, "even if what we do goes unacknowledged?"

"Especially if it goes unacknowledged!" Judith smiled

"I'd like that," Jim said, taking Judith by the hand. "To live for the sheer experience of being alive.

We felt small next to this giant flower and, although we hadn't said a word, we knew we were both suddenly filled with deep longing

9

Judith Sherven and James Sniechowski

Intimacy is like that, you know. When we allow ourselves to open and connect, intimacy can be an unexpected teacher, taking us into unacknowledged places in our self

Whenever any of us stops long enough to open, to feel the tenderness that is at the core of being alive, the magic of the mystery appears— right there, wherever we are

That little red flower became a portal, a threshold into the world of the ordinary and the sacred, into something completely expected and yet utterly surprising. That's the pleasure and the reward of real intimacy. It takes you through what you already know, out beyond your imagination

We stayed with that flower for some minutes, each in our own silence. And then, as though on cue, we rose, and walked hand in hand back to the house

There are opportunities all around you, right now, in your daily life, to let intimacy carry you into yourself and out toward those you love

Let it. Just say "yes," open your eyes, and let it.

...love is the most powerful and still the most unknown energy of the world.

--Pierre Teilhard de Chardin

5. LET GO OF THE HABITS OF CHILDHOOD

One of the markers of childhood is the need to have the environment—family, neighborhood, etc.—provide a sense of being alive. For example, mothers are constantly creating things for their children to do to keep them busy. So children learn to rely on what's outside of them as the source of their life. That's one way they learn to become intimate with their environment. They are children, after all, and have little internal sense of self upon which to rely

But as we grow up—chronologically, at least—our internal sense of self is supposed to emerge. But there's no guarantee of that happening. Many of us remain hooked to outside stimulation and cannot hear the whispered prodding of our own soul

Yet intimacy is about sharing what we're like inside and receiving what our partner shows about his or her inside. So how do we develop an inside, a sense of self from which we can have something to share, in order to be intimate

By "inside" we don't mean ideas you've learned from books or opinions you've snatched from someone else.

11

And we don't just mean feelings, which are indisputably yours—if you can recognize them, that is. A sense of self begins to grow when you decide to shift from the habit of looking out to others to stimulate you and begin to rely on your inner self

To do this, you must at first be quiet. Not just silent, but still. The craving for outside stimulation needs to cease being dominant

Initially it will feel as if nothing's happening, as if your life has just shut down. At this point many people panic and go looking for an energy fix. What they get is just energy. Perhaps high energy, such as one receives from loud music, but just energy

When things shut down, it's time to turn your attention inward and listen—with your imagination, your intuition, your sense perception. Become intimate with your presence in the world. If you persist, the quiet deepens and you will become more and more secure with your own internal landscape. And then the sweetest intimacy will open itself to you, an intimacy with your self, with others, with life, with God, with being. A sense of profound connectedness will emerge, a sense of the eternal in the mundane, of the extraordinary in the simplest events of your day. And you will feel a closeness that only poetry can begin to convey—a deep quiet closeness that is always present

Let go of the habits of childhood and step into your own soul.

The walls we build around us to keep out the sadness also keep out the joy.

--Jim Rohn

6. THE ANTIQUE CARPET RUNNER

No matter how much two people have in common, they will always be different in significant and in tiny ways. The question is, when your partner behaves in ways you don't like, do you feel free to speak up and deal with issues that bug you, hurt you, scare you? Or are you afraid that speaking up will threaten your relationship

If you fear that speaking up will make a problem too huge to resolve, then you are voting for your fear and your lack of value. Do you get that? Your fear won't let you engage in a discussion about changes that you want (and we ALL want some changes in the course of a long-term relationship), and you are insisting that you aren't worthy of having a voice—only your partner is to be valued

The other day Jim was touching up some paint on a chair rail molding he'd put up in our hallway upstairs — and he was standing on an antique carpet runner we'd just purchased at an auction here. When Judith saw this, she was horrified for fear of a paint spill and shocked Jim would take such a risk

"Jim, please don't ever leave anything valuable around

when you've got paint.

"I'm being careful," Jim answered

"OK, but most accidents happen when we're being careful," Judith replied. "Please don't do it.

In response Jim rolled up the rug and told Judith he wouldn't do it again because he wanted her to be comfortable and not worried

If Judith hadn't spoken up she would have stewed over how dumb Jim can be, how his parents were dumb not to teach him to protect things, and she would have continued to build a private case against Jim, little by little distrusting him more and more, undermining the relationship

That's the destructive power of not speaking up

Love works because it is based on a continually created relationship, in which both people are loved for who they are and feel safe to risk speaking up

Don't cheat your love by hiding your complaints or desires. It needs the fertilizer of your speaking up!

You must look into people, as well as at them.
--Lord Chesterfield

7. WHERE DO YOU GO?

One morning during our walk along the road we noticed Baron, the horse next door, anxiously ranging around his corral. He is a grey and white dappled stallion with beautiful eyes, large and brown. As beautiful as they are, they are a source of maddening frustration for him because tiny flies—called "no-see-ums" because they are hardly visible—hover around them, attracted to the moisture. So he keeps moving to get away, looking for a spot in his corral where he can finally be at ease, an ease that seems just out of reach

Aren't we all like Baron? Aren't we driven to find a "place" where we can be at ease

Our need for intimacy is like that. No matter where we go, we yearn for closeness. We yearn for the sustenance of relationship, because we are all creatures who dearly and deeply depend upon one another, not just for our daily bread but for what our souls need: to be seen, recognized, appreciated for who we are. And so we keep ranging around the corral of our lives, pushed along by a wordless need to find connection

And yet even in our most intimate moments there is still an echo of longing. We are called beyond what is by a

15

whisper that says, "There is more. Reach out. There is more." We have what we want and still there is more, and so the longing never recedes. Even though it can grow less intense, it never disappears completely

What do we so deeply long for? What can yield the ease that always seems just out of reach

Within every intimate moment there is the heartbeat of God. It doesn't matter what you understand God to be, we live with the sense that somewhere, someplace we will find home, a place we will finally be at ease

Intimacy is the doorway. Through intimacy your heart can touch and be touched, and as you listen very closely, there will be God—in your lover's eyes, in your own pulse, in the life that emerges when you let yourself be seen and known. And then God smiles and says, "Thank you. I've so dearly wanted to know you better.

There is a real and immediate sense of connection waiting for you and it's available everywhere, even in the eyes of a Baron living next door, who's trying to find his own place of ease. Open yourself and receive it. As you do, that face you glimpse out in the beyond may be God's and it may be your own. After all, aren't they really the same?

The supreme happiness in life is the conviction we are loved.
-Victor Hugo

8. THERE IS WISDOM IN YOUR CHOICE

There is great wisdom in your choice of serious love partners. Wisdom that doesn't always meet the eye. In fact, on the surface, it may seem as if the two of you are so different that you'll not even be able to make it. But with a full commitment to the totality of love, those very same differences will not only fertilize your relationship, keeping your lives vital and always changing, but will also spur you to greater personal growth

Yesterday Jim went into town for his morning newspaper and donut pick-up. On his way out Judith handed him a form to take to the library, so we could formally apply to use the civic center for a presentation we wanted to make

When he got back Judith asked how it went at the library. Jim looked surprised. He'd forgotten all about it and didn't even know where the form was! Well! In the early part of the marriage, when this ditzy side of Jim would show itself, Judith would usually flip out. She'd get angry and scared and start crying in total frustration!

Sometimes it would deteriorate into long, drawn-out fights as we struggled to find our equilibrium—because Jim never saw anything tragic going on and Judith always did

You see, Judith was raised in a family that took getting things done "right" very seriously. So she developed a perfectionist bent, coupled with a need to avoid "trouble" or getting into "trouble." (Can you identify with that?) That followed her into marriage and obviously caused a great deal of pain for both of us

The wisdom in marrying Jim is that today Jim is still prone to being ditzy, but Judith has learned from him that his "relaxed attitude" has never caused a catastrophe and so she has relaxed enormously and seldom gets upset anymore

That's not to say that Jim is so relaxed he's dangerous. We're talking about non-consequential issues. But it's often the little things that drive people into divorce court; they simply cannot tolerate each other's personal styles

Please remember—the other person is not you. Your partner is not you. That may sound obvious, even simplistic, but the next time you go off on your partner because he or she hasn't done something "right"—in other words, the way you would do it or the way it "should" be done—you are insisting there's only one person in the world and that is YOU! Intimacy takes two and it's most delicious when the two aren't the same. Then the adventure of love can be wondrous and your relationship can stay fresh and vital

18

Jim found the library form in his office. He'd been distracted and left it behind. He turned it in the next day. Judith didn't even skip a beat on this one and got to celebrate her cool attitude and tease Jim, in a loving way, about his "absent-minded professor" ways, which he didn't deny

We both had a good time on our walk today, talking about how much we've learned from one another and how grateful we are for it. That's what can happen when you learn the wisdom in your choice of each other

Take a look at all the ways your relationship, even if it didn't work out, was a very wise choice, in terms of all you've learned from it! And be grateful.

Judith Sherven and James Sniechowski

What we are losing as a culture is an awareness of the miracle of everyday life.
--Victor Nunez

9. CLASSICAL INTIMACY

Last Saturday night we went to a chamber music concert here in our small town. It was held in an historical church turned civic center, seating only 250. These world-class musicians were invited to play by fellow members of the NY Metropolitan Opera who live here, and were paid far less than they are accustomed to

Rather than holding back, assuming the small-town audience wouldn't know the difference, or protecting themselves from whatever inadequacies they might encounter (like having to wait in the tiny adjacent library before going on), they gave the most masterful performances we've ever seen in our lives! They played from their hearts and souls and they demanded with their very beings that we all follow them into the ecstatic passions that drove their spirited playing

You might imagine a rural audience would be polite, reserved in their appreciation for these musicians with foreign names, these players who pushed their instruments and bodies into an impassioned duet of epic astonishment. But no, these people in shorts and slacks leapt to their feet, screamed out their joy and showered a reciprocal intimacy right back upon those on stage

Judith was in tears much of the time, in awe of the unspeakable beauty made possible by the musicians' giving themselves to the larger forces of the music. Jim was swept up in a kind of cosmic oneness with all life, as he opened to the power and majesty of the playing. We held hands, made knowing eye contact, and shared the ecstasy together. Intimacy upon intimacy swept back and forth from stage to audience, and back again, transforming everyone

Intimacy is about opening yourself, entering the moment, eager to see what is calling you. How often do you open yourself that way to your marriage, your relationship, your date? How often do you open yourself fully to yourself, letting your soul speak to you, engaging intimately with what wants to be revealed within you

Like those musicians, intimates must practice. They must also surrender to the force of the flow between them. That's what leads to the heights and the depths of being together with someone. That's what makes the music of passion that we opened to last Saturday night and were filled

Please join us in saying yes to passion, yes to experience, yes to life!!!!!

Differences are the roots without which the tree of liberty, the sap of creation and of civilization, dries up.
--Albert Camus

10. THE REVEALING TOUCH

A number of years ago Jim challenged Judith, telling her she didn't touch him as much as he touched her. Judith was shocked. From her perspective, she was very affectionate physically. "No way," said Jim. "Not so.

By that time in our relationship we'd learned how to couch criticism so it wasn't experienced as an attack. Yet Jim wanted her to know he was very serious and meant it as a challenge, meant for her to become more aware, and, of course, much more physically affectionate

A short time later we were driving to meet her father, a trip of about an hour and a half. During the ride Judith asked, "Jim, do you feel that?" She was smiling.

"Feel what?" Jim said

Making her point, she squeezed his thigh where her hand already touched him. "That.

He looked down and immediately knew he had been hoisted on his own challenge. "How long has your hand been there?"

Judith was beaming with affection. "Oh, about three minutes." "Oh," he smiled, and began to move his mouth

22

as though he was chewing

"What are you doing?" Judith wondered

As a blush was rising in his cheeks, he half-whispered, "Well, this crow isn't bad. Your recipe?

We both laughed, enjoying each other's humanity

Sadly, in many relationships, such a moment has potential for real danger. The partner exposed for being unaware can feel it as humiliation and then retaliate. But that happens only when the foibles and frailties of being human are not embraced. The fact is, we all occasionally feel absolutely certain about something, only to bump into the wide scope of our own lack of awareness

You see, intimacy has a difficult time with absolute certainty. There's no room to breathe, no room to receive reality

Albert Camus wrote, "Nothing is true that forces one to exclude." We believe that wholeheartedly. Jim was not proclaiming from on high when he made the initial challenge. And Judith had no intention of belittling him. Reality was the point. Reality—the only place where penetrating intimacy can take root and become a spiritual bouquet

Keep in mind, this point is tricky. We all have powerful feelings and act on them with confidence. That's okay. As long as you remember not to exclude. When you do, you get caught in your own lie

Jim's challenge opened up more awareness for us both. And that's the point. Intimacy and awareness are two sides of the same soul. Besides, now very little, if any, of

23

our touching goes by unnoticed. That's one level of the payoff. The other is consciousness. We are much more

aware of each other's needs with regard to physical affection, giving and receiving it more freely and joyously

Don't back away from announcing what you believe is right. Even if it's not, if your intention is to support the well-being of your relationship, you will be rewarded in the end.

Perfect love means to love the one through whom one became unhappy.

--Soren Kierkagaard

11. THE BUG FUNERAL PARLOR

One of the wonders of being in a long-term relationship that celebrates "the magic of differences" is that you can divvy up the daily chores, errands, and family support requirements along the lines of each another's strengths and weaknesses, preferences and distastes

For instance, one ongoing challenge of country living is the BUGS! Big moths, black wasps, tiny "no-see-ums," and all manner of flies and critters figure out how to get inside our house. With a night light in our bathroom drawing everything in there after we turn out the lights, every morning the sink, floor and window become a bug funeral parlor

Judith finds these creatures obnoxious—alive or dead! Jim doesn't mind them most of the time and does most of the clean up in the bathroom. He actually enjoys saving the live ones with his hands or an empty plastic juice jug and a piece of cardboard, in which he traps the wasps for safe escort out of the house. So now Judith just calls out for "Bug Patrol!" and knows Jim will come rescue her

Respecting our differences allows Judith to feel taken

care of by Jim, and allows Jim to be the Bug Patrol General

In the old way of thinking about differences, we'd both be making each other wrong. Jim wouldn't hesitate to make fun of Judith for being so "prissy and girlie" and "overly sensitive." Judith would condemn Jim for being "macho" and "tough" and ignoring his "real feelings" of disgust. Each of us would feel righteous and correct— certain the other was wrong and deserved to be punished by verbal abuse

In the new intimacy the fun is in sharing life—and embracing all the ways our differences enhance one another and allow our individuality to shine

So remember: the other person you're involved with is not you. Remember the ways he or she is different from you can make your life easier, better, more fun. Rejoice in those differences!

When your illusions clash with reality, when your falsehoods clash with truth, then you have suffering.

--Anthony de Mello

12. LOVE IS TAKING YOU

Because there are two distinctly different people in any relationship—and as soon as you meet someone, there's a relationship—and because change, unceasing change, is a fundamental part of life, your relationship(s) will never stay firmly, predictably in place. Never, unless you both die emotionally and settle for Dullsville

When you really get this, or "grok" it, as Robert Heinlein said, then you can begin to enjoy and look forward to the many seasons your long-term relationships will go through

This is very similar to the flowing changes in the local wild flowers here. Since we arrived we've noted with excited pleasure the beginnings of the many different flowering weed species in their abundant blooming. A week or two later, some are fading, and altogether new shapes and colors and sizes are erupting with gleeful abandon. This riotous infusion of new life into the already living, and into the dying of that now beyond its time, brings us such delight as we take morning walks down our road

"Oh, look, we've never seen that kind!" "Well, there

are just a few of those left blooming." "What do you imagine we'll find next time?

We've speculated on what it would be like if they all came into their season at the same time. For one thing, it would be difficult to appreciate them as independently wonderful expressions of nature's creativity—they would all run wild over one another. And it would be all or nothing, with no progression and development to the spectacle

So many people want their relationships set in stone right from the beginning—no surprises, no growth, no unfolding. But life and love are not like that. The blessing of real-life love is that each of us keeps growing if we stay open to its lessons; then our relationships can never

be boring, never beyond improvement, never without further depths of love to discover

In our first book, The New Intimacy: Discovering the Magic at the Heart of Your Differences, we introduced the concept of "serial monogamy with the same person"—the continual unfolding, the expansive evolution in a long-term relationship, as both partners grow and change

Enjoy all the seasons, even when you are too hot, too cold, and even when your love life isn't going according to your private plan. At all times know that love is taking you where it needs you to go!

You must do the thing you cannot do.
--Eleanor Roosevelt

13. LIFE IS LIFE

Some people have said of our relationship that we seem to have an idyllic life, always in harmony, hassle-free. We want to make sure that myth is dispelled. Yes, we've been together for 19 years (married 18), we've resolved a lot of conflicts, and we know each other far better than we did in the beginning—but there are still times when the relationship and/or life is challenging, sometimes extremely so

For instance, each of us has hoped, from time to time, to find that perfect peace, a solid, unflappable self-confidence that would transform all of life into a kind of spiritual paradise. Even though we teach against this, it still looms up to bite us in the you know where.

Moving from the wilds of Santa Monica, CA to the wildly romantic mountainside of Windham, NY, where the country is soooo beautiful, captured both of us. Country life evoked the idea, largely unconscious, that living here would be THE answer. Windham country would bring total fulfillment—especially for Jim (Judith is still more a city girl and that helped her stay comparatively grounded)

As a result, a major and tender aspect of our current intimacy is now an ongoing conversation about the gradually fading honeymoon feeling of being here. Our recognition, once again, that there is no redemption, no secret solution to life's challenges, and absolutely no free lunch, connects us even more deeply with the fact that life is life. We must still dance with it as it is and we tweak our awareness daily to make certain we understand that not only is this life enough, it is an ongoing blessing

You may not think of that as intimate. True, it's not what happens in the movies. But it is deeply comforting and very trusting to share our secret wishes, our hope against hope that a kind of total redemption can be had

In its place we review all the blessings of our lives, including meeting one another on a blind date on March 7th, 1987. We continue to relish being here and rejoice in new experiences, such as picking our own blackberries, which grow wild in the back yard. And we work to grow more patient as the paperwork piles up on the floor, just like in our old place; as we grieve the lack of a good, handy dry cleaners; and as we drive almost an hour to have our copier fixed

Life is life. While we all have a lot of creative input on how it goes for us, at other times all we can do is surrender once again to life on its terms. Talking about your frustrations, your fading dreams, your wish that life could be different than it is can be a wondrously intimate time. Remember that you have each other, and give thanks for all that blesses your life together.

To feel truly a part of each other's lives, you'll have to make room in your territory, not just in your bed.

--Cheryl Merser

14. AS IS

We all come into our romantic relationships with old emotional baggage. A lot of it's so psychologically primitive it seems it should have no place in how we think and what we do as adults. And yet old fears, old insecurities, old desperations can sound their very powerful roars and stir up unpleasant, and sometimes self-destructive, feelings and behaviors

When we're not aware of this stuff our unconscious "junk" can ride roughshod over a marriage or long-term relationship, because our responses make no rational sense considering what is going on in the moment. But with a little compassion and conscious caring, what

we feel and do can make perfect sense when we understand it in the context of our past

A few weeks ago Judith's mouse (not the one in the kitchen, but her computer sidekick!) had a heart attack of some kind and was most unruly and hard to work with. For some reason the frustration touched an old nerve of feeling betrayed. So when Jim came in to ask a question, Judith was weeping in desperation, trying to make the mouse do her bidding

From Jim's perspective the dying mouse was a drag and could easily be replaced. Yet what about Judith's very real agony?

Jim's perspective was clearer because he doesn't share her issues. That's an example of the power and magic of the differences between us—between any two people committed to one another. He could stay centered emotionally while we tried to find the root of the problem

His gentle calmness was very comforting. Because we are committed to accepting one another "as is," what might seem like melodrama was treated with respect and in that way healed a bit

When we say we accept one another "as is," we mean that whatever we encounter in one another is the truth of the moment. Judith's weeping, no matter how disproportionate or out-of-the-present it was, was the truth. So we had to accept it "as is." That doesn't mean, however, that we don't desire change from one another. "As is" doesn't extend to unadulterated acceptance. To do that would be wholly unrealistic, to say nothing of unhelpful. But at the same time no one can demand we be who we're not

If Jim said, "Judith, don't be ridiculous, you should be having a different response," he would have been self-centered to say nothing of cruel. We accept each other "as is" as the starting point and work for change from there, out of a respect for what is going on—no matter how distorted that "going on" may be

Judith's weeping stemmed from difficulties she experienced as a child with being dependent and feeling unsafe in the world—those early fears translated into feeling violated when her trusty computer "betrayed" her. The "crisis" opened up new territory to be understood by both of us. We both got to explore even deeper levels of intimacy centered around the issue of fearing neediness and being dependent, while also solving the very un-psychological problem of fixing the mouse, at least enough to make it work until it was replaced

What old issues come up and haunt your current relationship? How can you use the ways you are different from your partner to help ease his or her pain, fear, anger, whatever? How can you relate to old emotional baggage as a source for deeper knowing of one another, rather than feeling overwhelmed or burdened

When you open to one another "as is," and work to grow from there, the rewards of your becoming more and more intimate will be well worth the time and "trouble."

Judith Sherven and James Sniechowski

Be yourself, no matter what.
You mustn't act a certain way because you are
afraid of an adverse reaction.
--Martha Stewart

15. LOVE ISN'T BEING ALIKE

Sometimes the most difficult thing to remember is
that your beloved is not you. Your sweetheart cleans up
the kitchen, but not to your specifications. You're upset
and you file your complaint. You find yourself exclaiming,
"I wouldn't have done it that way!!!!!!," as if your way is the
only way

The problem is that so many of us were raised in
families where there was only one right way to think, feel,
and behave. Unless we become conscious of how stifling it
was, we then try to force the same demands onto our
partner—all in the name of love. But love between equals
requires that we give up insisting on one way to be, one
way to feel, and open ourselves to the one we say we love,
to truly honor their reality, as well as our own

We met a man today at a yoga class get-together and
he remarked how, now that he's retired, he loves to stay at
home and bask in the sight of the Black Dome Mountains.
At the same time his wife loves to travel, so he encourages
her to travel with friends and was so pleased she'd found
the yoga group to get out and enjoy

A friend of ours loves to "moon bathe"—basking nude out on his deck or lawn. His wife is far more modest, so she joins him fully clothed and appoints herself the lookout, so she can throw a towel over him if car lights appear

Jim believes in the death penalty. Judith doesn't. Judith is certain there's some kind of God. Jim's not sure. Jim loves football. Judith could care less. Judith loves leftovers. Jim doesn't like them

Love isn't based on being alike (that's just an outer manifestation of self-centered narcissism). While being alike is comforting and fun, love asks that we stretch beyond ourselves to embrace the difference of the one we say we love. It also requires that we hang on to our own unique identity and not get lost trying to please the other person by becoming invisible, so as to appear just like they are

Take a real good look at someone you love and notice how he or she is not like you. Identify all the aspects you can. And then focus on what you'd miss if they turned into a carbon copy of you. Isn't it great they are not you?!

To handle yourself, use your head;
to handle others, use your heart.
--Proverb

16. THE INSIDE-OUT SOCK

To accurately understand relationship dynamics, it is essential to appreciate that two people are always co-creating a relationship—and that this process begins the moment they meet. They indicate what they like and what they don't, what they will put up with or not, how generous they are—emotionally, spiritually, monetarily, or not—they speak up for themselves or they don't, and they receive the goodness coming their way or they can't

This give and take goes on throughout the life of any relationship, either in the service of the love two people share or in the service of undermining it

For example, until we moved here to our country home in Windham, we've always had someone who cleaned for us and did our laundry. Here, so far, we find we like doing it all ourselves. Jim has been in the habit of pulling off his socks inside out and wearing them that way if not corrected by someone else (you see, not only does he not care, he just doesn't notice it!). Judith hates seeing him looking like the absent- minded professor, though we agree he is from time to time! And she is now doing the laundry. So early on here in Windham, she asked Jim to please be sure to put his socks into the laundry basket right side out

If she hadn't asked, Jim would never have known this was an issue for her. AND she would have been annoyed every time she "had to" turn them right-side-out. Thus she showed her love for herself and for Jim in the request. Jim could have refused and ignored the impact on her, which would have violated his love for her (and for the relationship). His other option was to respect that Judith has a thing about socks being right-side-out that he doesn't, and agree to her request, thereby showing his love every time he flips his socks around

A simple example, right? Even a bit simplistic? But it's just these kinds of issues that simmer over time, then boil over into marriage-breaking catastrophes

Now Judith feels loved every time she folds Jim's right-side-out socks and Jim feels loving every time he turns them right-side-out before putting them in the basket. You might still be saying, "What's the big deal?!!" But it is precisely this ignorance of such issues, the ignoring of daily irritations, that robs love of its wonder and joy

Genuine love is always a two-way dance, an ongoing collaboration in consideration of yourself and the other person. If you are feeling victimized in your relationship, please look to see how you are allowing it. If you feel you are falsely accused of being the "cause" of all the problems, please notice how you've allowed that idea to develop

37

It's never too late to change how the two of you express your power with, and care for, one another. Just be sure you see that you both share the power, no matter how you use it or what it looks like

on the surface. Please use it well and in the service of connection, understanding, and respectful caring of yourself and one another.

There is no remedy for love but to love more.
--Henry David Thoreau

17. BUGS ARE BEINGS TOO!

Most of the time we write about how to respect and value the differences between you and the one you love. Of course, that point of view will spill over onto all the other people you encounter once the magic of differences is firmly stashed away in your awareness. Then your life becomes much fuller, far less adversarial, and your everyday experience is a kind of practical spirituality

Now we'd like to enlarge the picture of what your new intimacy can contain—namely, a deeper respect and value for all of nature. We're not going to say you should never kill a fly or avoid meat. That's a personal decision. Admittedly, for all the moths and spiders and wasps we've caught and released outdoors with our plastic apple juice "bug catcher," we've also swatted flies and killed other bugs as they flew into our halogen lamps or our less-than-effective blue-light bug machine (now returned)

Yet the point we want to make is that in a new intimacy with nature, both the killing (when the ants have taken over your kitchen, for example) and the rescue can be powerfully spiritual experiences, as long as you pay attention to the relationship you are having with the being over which you have control. Bugs are beings too! (Even

Judith Sherven and James Sniechowski

though some of them drive Judith crazy on warm summer nights here in the country.

When we take our morning walks down our road, from time to time we encounter little orange lizards and small frogs out sunning themselves on the pavement. It's become our habit, initiated by Jim, to stop and either shoo them off into the brush, or pick them up and place them in the wild grasses where the cars won't run over them. In this way, we pay respect to our animal relations, and the two of us are joined in a very intimate rescue mission. It's real romance and it's a "thank you" to Creation for all that is here

How can you enlarge your relationship with nature and, at the same time, enjoy a richness of intimacy with your sweetheart?

Love is like a diamond, the hardest and purest of all minerals, able to scratch anything, yet nothing can scratch it.

--Fidel Castro

18. WHAT SHALL WE DISCOVER

It's said that every morning Pablo Casals, the world-famous cellist, asked his cello, "My dear friend, what shall we discover together today?" Not what they would do separately, but together, communicating with each other, calling on the best both had to offer

They were an extension of each other, yet neither one disappeared. By joining together, yet remaining distinct, they became something more than the sum of the parts. They became a single creative voice—impossible without both of them. They depended upon one another to transcend their individual limitations, in order to create exquisite music. Their music was an expression of what is possible from a disciplined, open, and loving collaboration

This morning we went out for a walk. Jim's mother is arriving in the morning for a visit and we wanted to pick wild flowers for her. Jim carried the scissors and leapt across the rain run-off ditches and Judith carried whatever flowers we cut. Back at home we stood, side by side, at the kitchen sink, placing the flowers in five different vases. We could buy flowers at a local florist, but then the collaboration that is manifested in our displays would be absent

The fact that the flowers are wild is also part of the expression. This will tell his mother that we took the time and care to pick them for her

Because we're in mid-September, most of the wild flowers have receded, so our walk became a real discovery. But that's what made it fun

A relationship is a single creative voice. It is more than the two, impossible if one is missing. The two depend on each other, trusting they will both transcend their individual limitations, knowing that neither one will disappear. Then, like Casals and his cello, they create a unity never before heard in the world

How do you live your relationship? When you wake in the morning, say to your partner, "My dear beloved, what shall we discover together today?" There is an adventure awaiting you both, if you surrender to your love. Then your relationship serves as a sacred instrument, allowing you to discover and express your individual—and mutual— spirit and grace.

If people see the lowly side of their own natures, they will also learn to understand and love others better.

--Carl Jung

19. CURIOSITY

What's one of the sexiest things you can do? What thrills the one you love more than anything? And what brings you into the deepest connection of knowing one another? What is it? It's curiosity!

What could be sexier than the one you love sincerely wanting to know you better, wanting to understand your different point of view, wanting to learn more about your childhood, wanting to understand the way you tick in the specifically fascinating ways you do. In the ways that only you do

Wow! You're not being taken for granted! You're not getting an argument. Instead you're being asked to explain your position on the subject at hand. And you're really being heard. Your lover is listening with his or her entire heart and soul. You are being respected and valued for the unique individual that you are

We've been together 19 years, married 18, and we are still delighting in discovering new stuff about each other

This morning we saw a white fuzzy caterpillar crossing the road while we were out for our walk. It was clear it needed to be rescued and put in the bushes, but

Judith didn't move to do it, even though she saw the critter first. So, rather than decide she was being a princess (which she can be!), Jim asked why she waited for him to do the job

"I developed a real yucky response to caterpillars when I was a kid. The neighbor's tree that overhung our driveway would get saturated with really prickly ugly caterpillars and they'd fall off onto our driveway— and your head if you weren't careful. They revolted me and I still respond that way to all caterpillars, even though this one is pretty cute. So I really appreciate you picking it up.

We felt more connected, more intimate, and we knew more about each other, all because of one question

What can you ask your partner about? Pay attention, there's always something that can bring you a big dose of the new intimacy—it's yours for the asking!

Judith Sherven and James Sniechowski

People prefer to live in a huge asylum, religiously following rules written by who knows whom, rather than fight for the right to be different.
--Paulo Coehlo

20. SEPARATE AND DISTINCT

What do you want more than anything in the world? We suspect it's to be seen, valued, and loved for all that you are. Think of it: all that you are! Not just the funny parts, the nice parts, the generous parts. But also the crabby parts, the worried parts, the physically sick parts, the depressed parts, the "dumb" parts. Have you ever had that kind of love

Most people didn't grow up with it. Their parents weren't full enough inside themselves, and within their own life experience, to know how to do that for them. Consequently we often have trouble knowing it's even possible to be loved that way

So that's why we write about the new intimacy, why we give 366 different ways to experience it in our second book, Opening to Love 365

Days a Year. Being loved for all that we are is a very new concept and is only possible when we recognize one another as different, unique, and unfinished

When we met on a blind date in 1987, part of our dinner conversation was about how we were both dissatisfied with aspects of our work

At 45 Jim had been married twice before and at 43 Judith had never married. Hardly the stuff of a modern romance novel. Yet we were open to exploring the reality of what we each brought to our meeting. Thirteen months later we were married and working together to bring spiritual awareness to the ways we can all experience intimacy through our differences

Too often love never has a chance to grow and develop because the lovers insist it be perfect right from the beginning. Well, that's impossible, unless you see the foibles, limitations, and excellences in your partner as exactly the right stuff to help you expand the way you know to love, as just the right catalyst for your spiritual growth. When you both feel this way, and are willing to do the internal and joined "lovework" to create a wonderful, ongoing intimacy, then it is perfect

Only then can you both be loved for who you are individually, separate and distinct from each other.

An injury is big or little according to the degree of sensitiveness that receives it.

--Arthur Henry

21. THAT STUPID STUFF

In the old intimacy it seemed it was fair game to chastise your lover or spouse for the ways in which he or she was different from you—ways that made you mad, upset you, scared you. It was okay to roll your eyes in contempt, or to be sarcastic as you told your kids how your spouse had been such a goofus earlier that day. All you were expected to do, in relation to these annoying differences, was to "tolerate" them

But we don't want to be tolerated. Do you? Probably not! Thus in the new intimacy we look for the "magic" in the differences, even when that magic is hard to find. By magic we mean the greater significance, the exciting opportunity to learn more about yourself and/or one another. Sometimes the magic is just the freedom to laugh rather than get mad. Or, if you can't laugh, to at least be compassionate—that's magic too. Especially when you're on the receiving end

A couple of weeks ago Jim carried a lamp upstairs with the glass shade still on—or it was until it hit the low ceiling and shattered, falling all over the landing and down the stairs

Judith was in the dining room downstairs reading the paper when she heard the awful, telling sound. But the instant she felt angry at Jim's "stupidity," she remembered. Remembered not to be nice, not to be silent, not to tolerate. No, she remembered that she, too, has been perfectly "stupid" in her ways. Like the time she backed the car out of the garage too close to the wall and whacked the side mirror right off. Or the time she forgot to turn off the boiling eggs and had to call home from the hair dressers to have Jim save the pan (the eggs were hopeless!)

There is wonderful magic when we remember we are all, in many ways, perfectly imperfectly human. And only then can we meet one another in the heart of compassion, in the grace of oneness—only when we value and respect each other's differing ways of being "stupid." Then we can be intimate, helping to clean up the broken glass, reminding the one we love there's no need to feel guilty. Because everyone—yes, everyone—does stuff that's "stupid."

If at first the idea is not absurd, then there is no hope for it.

--Einstein

22. ONE, TWO, THREE, CLICK

Lately we've been taking lots and lots of photos—of our house, our yard and pond, the fall foliage, the first snow. It's sort of a documentary to show Judith's father all the aspects of where we live. As a result we've noticed how differently we prepare to take a photo! Judith counts: "One…two…three" and then click

Jim describes her technique this way: "One. Two. Three. Pause. Four. Five (whispered). Click!!!

Jim's style? "One, two, three click!" The three and the click happen simultaneously

No big deal, you say?! Welllll…it is if you're trying for a natural pose and you think the timing is YOUR timing…and it's NOT

In the old intimacy we'd be fighting over who's "right" and who's "wrong." We'd be lost in a power struggle that could destroy our love and our relationship. All over the "proper" countdown for snapping photos. Because there could only be ONE right way

Instead, we joke about it and tease each other when we are getting ready for the photos—and they're coming out even cuter and sillier because we're having such a good time goofing around together

After all, there's no RIGHT way to count before taking a photo. Just an opportunity to get to know each other better and to have more fun figuring out how to enjoy the differences!!

One. Two. Three. Don't forget the pause. Four. Five. Click!!!! One. Two. Three. Click!!!

Ah, those differences.

People cannot discover new lands until they have the courage to lose sight of the shore.

--André Gide

23. SPIDER SAVERS AND DEER HUNTERS

Intimacy often arrives in forms we don't expect, especially when we come face to face with something about ourselves and cannot look away. Sometimes that's not so pleasant. At other times it can be a lesson about how we relate to the differences between us and others

Recently, Jim was cleaning the bathrooms. In the downstairs shower he found a spider that had fallen into the tub; because of the smooth porcelain, it couldn't crawl out. So he went to the garage where we keep an empty plastic apple juice jar and a piece of cardboard from the back of a yellow pad. We use that to catch moths, hornets, or insects we find indoors. Usually they're on the windows trying to get out. We scoop them up and release them

He caught the spider and was heading outside to put the spider in the weeds. Once in the garage he could see, in the field next to our home, a local man he'd met a few days before—a man now dressed in fatigues, bow strapped over his shoulder, heading out to hunt the deer now in season. The contrast was stunning. Jim delivering a spider to freedom. The other man hoping to end a deer's life

At first Jim felt self-righteous. He'd made the better choice. He was the more conscious of the two men. But a moment's thought brought the reality of the hunter's choice into focus. The hunter was not going to kill indiscriminately. Part of the winter economy of some residents in our area consists of meat they bring home during the hunting season. That man was providing for his family

Who was the better? What a simpleminded question. How could the idea of "better" even apply? Each was following through with what he believed. Neither was violating his integrity. Neither intended malice

If we keep ourselves open to what life brings, we grow more and more aware of our own beliefs and judgments. We may never walk directly in another person's shoes, but if we stay open, willing to embrace the differences between us, we come near enough to embrace those whose ways seem unfamiliar

In truth, we are all more alike than we are willing to admit. If we stay closed, we cast judgment on others and call judgment down on ourselves. If we stay open, we embrace those who are not like us, and make ourselves available to be embraced in turn

Spider savers and deer hunters. Different in appearance only. Underneath, pretty much the same

That is the magic waiting for us when we let each other be who we are, and see the world in the vast variety that is the signature statement of Creation.

I realize today that nothing in the world is more distasteful to a man than to take the path that leads to himself.

--Hermann Hesse

24. TWO HEADS: DEFINITELY BETTER THAN ONE

Traditionally, it was assumed that only one person could make decisions—either for a couple or a group—and it was believed that person had to be a man. Women were expected to agree and submit to the man's "greater authority." But, as we know, women have broken out of that second-rank role. In the new intimacy men and women work together to co-create solutions to problems, so that both feel empowered and satisfied

That's how it was for us last week when we were bumped off a flight home, from Dulles to Albany. They'd downsized the plane, and only 29 of the 53 scheduled passengers could go. It was fine for us, but not for a young woman whose sister was getting married the next day. She was told that even though she had a boarding pass, which she'd arrived early to be sure to get, she did not step up when the boarding announcement was made, so they gave her seat to someone else. When she was told she burst into tears and was crying hysterically, as the best the airline could offer was a flight the next morning, which would cause her to miss her sister's wedding

Judith wasn't having any of that. She went to the gate counter and insisted that someone get on the plane and describe this woman's plight, to influence someone to volunteer to give up their seat. She was told that "rules and regs won't allow that," yet Judith assumed her own authority and continued to insist—loudly—drawing the 20 or so people who had been bumped into a circle of supporters for the young woman

Jim wasn't going to allow rules and regs to prevent this woman from getting on the plane, so he went to the supervisor's office and demanded action, walking with the supervisor to the gate and explaining the critical nature of the problem

The supervisor convinced a woman on the plane who'd purchased a ticket for her small child to hold the child on her lap. To compensate her, he gave her airline travel credits which amounted to two coast-to-coast round trips

The young woman, still sniffling, was escorted to the plane as we all clapped and cheered

Men and women assuming their individual authority worked together to make something happen. We never talked with one another, yet we functioned as a determined team, deciding by our actions how to proceed, committed to persisting together until we'd succeeded in our mission

That is what is now available to a man and a women, both capable of being decisive, both empowered to act on

Judith Sherven and James Sniechowski

their decisions, and both depending on the other to bring value and action into the world. The new intimacy recognizes that two heads are definitely better than one.

One reason why we have so much trouble with relationship today may be . . . we expect to find intimacy naturally, without education or initiation.

--Thomas Moore

25. DANCING AT THE FRINGE

Sad to say, many of us were raised to order marriages and family life in a well-regulated and predictable fashion. And then, lo and behold, life seems boring and tedious

But what about opening our lives and love to the unexpected, the mysterious? Such as the concept some people refer to as "Quantum Reality." In the quantum world of subatomic physics, it is now known that electrons don't move in a straight line, but leap from one energy level to another. Here, in the world at human size, events are no longer thought to be compressed into linear routes—B always follows A, C necessarily follows B, etc. The universe has revealed new secrets that tell us A can be followed by M, which can be followed by C and so forth—so we hold our minds open to the adventure of discovery

For example, we came to live here in the cozy, small town of Windham, New York, more through whim and a sense of destiny, than through any well-ordered plan. In fact, our moving here from Santa Monica made no sense on paper, and when our friends asked why we were doing it, our initial response was, "God's whim!

Now that we've been here almost seven months, we can see it has been one of the wisest "impulses" we've ever had. More than anything, the move to this entirely new type of environment broke us loose from many ingrained habits, making room for just the kind of things that can only happen when you trust the voyage you are on and look forward to the discovery it has in store for you

And it all happened because of a seeming disaster. We were in Manhattan during Valentine's Day week of 1999 to promote our book, The New Intimacy, on TV and radio. After doing "The View" we were bumped from everything

else—preempted because the Clinton impeachment findings were going to be announced! A disaster!!!! Right

Wrong!!! We took the time to travel by Amtrak to visit our friends Art and Pat who lived very near Windham, and we fell in love with the area. Rather than resist, rather than say "This is not logical," which on paper

58

it wasn't, we opened to it, and that was the leap that opened the new direction of our life together

Open yourself to the possibility of dancing at the fringes of what you already know and do, the reality you've constructed and live within, inviting the unimagined to grace your relationship, to bless your capacity to love. Give it a try. It works!

Since love is the most delicate and total act of a soul, it will reflect the state and nature of the soul....
--Jose Ortega Y Gasset

26. THE BEAUTY IN THE MOMENT

Winter is setting in here in the mountains. The trees have dropped their leaves, the grass isn't growing, frost is a regular morning visitor, and ice is not too far away. It's almost past remembering that the hills and pastures here were bursting with wild flowers just a few short months ago

But the lush, verdant summer is only one season, like lusty passion is only one expression in the life of a relationship. Things change, and sometimes the beauty is not immediately apparent

As we walk along the road the winter colors are muted and unassuming. We can't rely on them to excite us. Instead, we have to give more of ourselves, we have to open and extend ourselves. We have to bring more to the exchange because one half of the partnership—the winter landscape—doesn't have the energy it once did

Love is like that. Sometimes our partner doesn't have it to turn us on. Sometimes they don't feel well. Sometimes they're depressed. Sometimes they just want to be quiet. They're muted and withdrawn

That's when we have to extend ourselves, our sensitivity, and look for the beauty of the moment. It won't leap out and grab us, but it's there. And it doesn't mean there's anything we have to do but be respectful

of what's happening and, as in the winter, open to what it has to offer. It will return the rich gifts of its season and, after a time, will be wild flowers again.

Judith Sherven and James Sniechowski

Not a day passes when I haven't rid myself of another comfortable illusion.

--Nietsche

27. THE PAYOFF WAS A KISS

Sometimes what we write ends up with a few typos. Ordinarily Judith proofreads the final writing, and she's pretty good at spotting those critters. But one time we were under a deadline. Judith had gone to bed and fallen asleep before Jim had finished the piece we'd been working on. So he sent it out without her proofing it, but having "read every word" himself, as he told her the next day, assuring her she would not find a single typo

Knowing that Jim can't spot typos very well, she said, "What do I get if I find any?" Notice, that could have been the opening to a fight, since she was saying she couldn't trust him. Instead, Jim answered, "A kiss!

Who could get upset over that!!?

Sure enough, there, in the second line of the first paragraph, was the first typo—"tress" instead of "trees.

In the past Judith would've been angry. But with a kiss waiting in the wings, she just ran to Jim's office and collected! Then there was a second kiss. And then, when she went in for the third (and final) kiss, Jim was screaming with mock embarrassment and hiding behind some papers. So we got to laugh and then Judith collected

62

her final missed-typo kiss

The key here is that we were on the same team. We didn't need to have WW III over this. As long as we were conscious, we could celebrate our closeness and seal it with kisses

Your relationship is far more important than saying "I told you so." There's no need for rage or punishment or vengeance. Just don't forget to enjoy the fun as you creatively avoid these pitfalls!

Judith Sherven and James Sniechowski

Love is something that grows by sharing our imperfect inner worlds.

John Amodeo

28. THE INTIMACY OF CRITICISM

It the heart of a loving relationship is concern for each other's well-being. However, that doesn't always take the form of tenderness and affection. Sometimes being critical is as loving as anything we might otherwise do

Some of you may already be taking exception. You may be thinking that criticism can only be negative. That's understandable. Most criticism is negative, and is usually meant to promote the "virtues" and advance the status of the critic. The receiver is often left emotionally bloodied and then expected to change for the better

Then there's what's called "constructive criticism," which often means the critic can get away with it because he or she claims it is for the betterment of the person whose "faults" are being "improved." Then the receiver is left in need of emotional convalescence

But criticism can also mean loving and careful judgment. When delivered with the well-being of the receiver truly in mind, loving criticism can inspire a turning point, and be as devoted as anything else we can give

For example, bring to mind a time when you saw

someone you loved engage in a behavior that was self-destructive. It could have been drugs, or maybe lack of commitment to an important project. It could have been weight or self-pity or anything that made the person less than you knew they could be. What was your loving obligation to that person

We are all deeply dependent upon one another to be there when we get lost. That is especially true between intimates

When we do our radio show, Jim has an unconscious habit of cracking his knuckles. It happens only every now and then, but it happens. When Judith asked him why, at first he felt attacked

"Nobody can hear it," he protested

"That's not the point," Judith cautioned. "It's that you're unconscious about it.

She was right and he couldn't deny it. So why did he do it

After he thought about it he realized it was a way of expending excess energy. But rather than dissipating his focus, she urged him to take that energy and put it into what he was doing. It worked. His concentration heightened, he was even more observant and his delivery had more purpose to it

Was it criticism? Certainly. But was it also careful judgment? Without a doubt. And why? Because she had his best interests at heart and

was devoted enough to what she knew he wanted to

bring it to his attention. That forced him to be more conscious, which was a small, but important, turning point in his work on the air

When love is leading your actions, you need not be afraid of criticism. When it's well intended and well received, it yields gratitude and an even deeper intimacy.

Young people, who are beginners in everything, cannot yet know love: they have to learn it.
--Ranier Maria Rilke

29. DOING LOVE

We went away for Thanksgiving to visit Judith's brother and his family, and we returned to find that the temperature had been in single digits, the coldest so far that year

We also returned to find the pipe from our well was clogged with ice, and so we had very little water pressure. That means very little water

So Jim set about pouring hot water on the pipe, which thawed it enough to produce full, normal water pressure. Then he sruffed fiberglass insulation around the pipe which kept it from freezing again

We also discovered the drain from the kitchen sink was blocked. When we tried to plunge it free, we somehow created a siphon which drew water back into the sink basin

Before going to bed that night, Judith was concerned that the sink might overflow and flood the kitchen. Jim thought it was unlikely

When we awoke in the morning there was, standing on the kitchen counters, an assortment of twelve containers—pots, bowls, pans, and one bucket—filled with cold, clear water. Judith had been right. Our mysterious siphon kept drawing all night and, because of her concern, she awoke twice during the night and each time found herself bailing out the sink in the kitchen

We both bailed until the plumber arrived and fixed the problem

But the mystery of how we had "engineered" the siphon effect went unresolved

It's easy to think about, talk about, and wish for, love. But doing love is not something we hear a lot about. It's true that love is a feeling or a sentiment, and that's important. But love is also, and more often, an action. Do love

Jim: Judith didn't wake me during the night. She did her love and left it for me to be surprised by the next morning

Judith: Jim didn't ask me to crawl into the utility shed with him, or get on my hands and knees to deal with the well-pipe. He did his love by doing what had to be done

And neither of us complained or bragged about what we did

It's so easy to take for granted the little things we do for one another. But if you include in your understanding of love that love is also an action, then love becomes evident all around you in all the things that are done for you every day—at the supermarket when the clerk takes extra care in bagging your groceries; or at the bank when the teller corrects your addition, giving you more in your deposit than you'd calculated; and, of course, when your lover does, without calling attention to it, all the little things he or she does that are just part of the way you live together

Love is expressed in action. Don't let the little things go unappreciated. Life is so much richer than many of us think.

Judith Sherven and James Sniechowski

Can I see another's woe, And not be in sorrow too?
--William Blake

30. POSSESSIVE OR INSISTENT

When we wrote our third book, Be Loved for Who
You Really Are, Judith was the lead writer and Jim did the
editing and first rewrite. It's a method that works well for
us. Both points of view are integrated so that neither of us
feels left out

Jim: One day I approached Judith for clarification
with regard to a phrase she'd written. I didn't know what
she was saying. Specifically, she'd used the word
"possessive." The context was no help, and so I needed to
talk with her

Judith: I tried to explain what I was doing, but from
Jim's point of view the word "insistent" was more
appropriate. We went back and forth a bit, and it was clear
we weren't getting anywhere except more frustrated

We were each embedded in our own worlds, trying to
convince the other of the rightness of our position. Rather
than being separate, we were isolated, detached and stuck,
and in a very real sense invisible to one another. We were
unable to respect that the two words, possessive and
insistent, were not a mere problem of semantics, but
represented subtly distinct experiences we were trying to
express

As curious as it may sound, it takes two to be separate. But only one to be isolated. When we realized we should be talking about our two distinct experiences rather than the meaning of words, we were able to see what the other meant. We still didn't agree, and in that sense remained distinct, but we were connected in our appreciation of the other's individuality.

A relationship cannot be successful unless there are two distinct persons recognizing each other across the chasms of their differences. Otherwise there are only two isolates co-habiting the same space.

Do not fear the differences between you. Embrace them. Sometimes they will cause friction and even conflict. But if you hold the well- being of your relationship as your first priority, you will need each other to create what you have. Then your relationship will truly reflect who you both actually are, in the mutual endeavor to which you have committed. And in that sense there will be a separation, an acknowledgment that the one you love is an "other," a separate being, full in his or her own integrity, a thrill to love and be loved by.

Judith Sherven and James Sniechowski

Age does not protect you from love. But love, to some extent, protects you from age.

--Jeanne Moreau

31. THE MIRACULOUS MYSTERY OF WINTER

Mystery can be fun. By mystery we don't mean that which is difficult, perhaps very difficult, but ultimately explainable. Rather we mean the deep, rich, and beguiling unknown that forms a backdrop for this life we all share

Late December into early January is that time when we in the northern hemisphere celebrate the miraculous. The miracle takes a variety of forms

Some celebrate nature's receding into the dark underground to slumber near the root of its own regeneration

Others sing about the birth of a redeemer, the ManGod whose arrival is a marvel that draws even kings to his cradle

Still others feel the need to reflect on the year past, to cleanse themselves of wrongdoing and to make amends to those they've wronged

When this time of year is taken seriously, the awesome mystery of life cannot be avoided

There is yet another mystery that is very near. It awaits us in the presence of the one we love. Imagine it:

this other person, almost an entire universe in his or her own right, a soul-radiance that continues to unfold before our very eyes. Could anything be more wonder-filled? And the magic in the mystery, which reveals itself when we open to it, when we relax into it, is that suddenly all living things become a miracle, especially those with whom we are most intimate

Give the gift of your full attention and allow yourself to be moved by the miracle of the one you love. You'll find that the lush mystery of simply being alive is poised, waiting to resound through you, through both of you, like a chorus of angels.

Judith Sherven and James Sniechowski

> We are what we think,
> having become what we thought.
> --Buddhist saying

32. WHY IS IT SO HARD TO ASK

New Year's Eve has passed. You're waking up to a new year. Maybe you'll watch the Rose Bowl Parade together. Perhaps you're giving a football party or having friends over for brunch

At the end of the day, you might want to spend some private, romantic time together sharing your dreams for the new year. What do you want? Each, individually? And both, together? Don't forget to talk about the things you desire that make you feel fearful, anxious, challenged, and/or in need of help and support from your partner

Something we talked about one year was our mutual desire to clean up our eating habits, asking each other for support. We even appointed each other to act as watch dogs! Limited potato chips for Jim and hardly any wheat for Judith. Ice cream only on rare occasions for both of us. Those were the major stumbling blocks. The rest we pretty well managed on our own

Notice how vulnerable and intimate it is to ask your love to help you clean up your act

It's sad that so many people have such trouble asking for help. They're so afraid they will lose themselves and

74

become a pawn of the person they need. But we all need. Everyday. This life would be impossible if we weren't supported by those we know—or even those we simply pass in our daily rounds

We want to expand the ways we get out our message about "The Magic of Differences," finding more outlets and methods of reaching singles and couples who want more spiritual meaning from their dating and committed relationships. We'll brainstorm together and play with new ideas. And yes, we'll no doubt stumble into our own anxieties. Will it work? Dare we ask? How will it look? Then we'll hold one another, physically and emotionally, and use our differences to challenge and support each other

Open yourselves to the future. Know you can be there for each other through it all, no matter what comes up. As long as you remember that the spiritual purpose for your being together is to more fully be who you are—both of you—and in that way expand your capacity to love, then you can go for it!!!

I have always been sorry/Our words were so trivial
And never matched the depths/Of our thoughts.
--Liu Yu Hsi

33. IN CONTACT

When you think of intimacy, what's the first image
that comes to mind? For some people it's sex. For others
it's deep communication. For others it can be the pristine
stillness of a mountain lake. What about feeling intimate
with those who lived in the past, say five or six hundred
years ago? No, we're not talking about time travel, at least
not in the science-fiction sense

We spent one vacation in Rome and visited a number
of churches and cathedrals. Some of those churches dated
back to the 13th and

14th centuries, magnificent structures that people use
for a variety of worship services. There are the famous
ones—Saint Peter's Basilica, the cathedral of Saint Maria
Maggiore, the Church of Saint John Lateran. But, one
afternoon we stumbled into the Chiesa del Gesu and were
struck with powerful awe, so much so that we could do
nothing but stand and gape

As in all the churches, the walls and ceiling were
covered with extraordinary frescoes, alive with compelling
and resounding colors. There was such a throbbing and
vital life depicted in the pictures, but even more so in the

consciousness they exuded, the spirit of the times in which they were painted

What struck us was how visceral the paintings were. Fleshy bodies, vivid colors, pulsing gestures, and an enthusiasm that radiated like light. There was no way we could have not felt the excitement and fervor of the artists, whose genius emanated from their work as much last week as when it was done hundreds of years ago. Those men were still alive, and we could feel them

Yes, their scenes were all religious. That was the content of the times. But more so, their excitement, their vision, their joy and their love burst through their work and filled us. We were in contact. We wondered what their lives must have been like, and they told us—not through the religious details, but through the wonder and ecstasy they experienced to communicate with the power they did

We were transported into their experience and both of us, independently, felt a sense of lifting off. That is a form of intimacy

Intimacy is a doorway into the abundance of life. You can experience that abundance sexually, emotionally, intellectually, spiritually and you can experience it with those who have lived and passed on if they have left behind something in which they invested their heart and soul

Please don't assume intimacy is limited to just you and your beloved. Expand your vision of what is possible and, when you do, the intimacy between you and the one you love will be deepened, sweetened, and enriched

Judith Sherven and James Sniechowski

because you will bring to it the currents, the vastness, of
life itself.

One of life's curious paradoxes is that you can't have intimacy without boundaries that define and protect your autonomy.

--John Amodeo

34. LOVE IS LIKE GRAVITY

The marriage ceremony asks two people to commit to loving each other "for better and for worse." It doesn't say "for better or for worse." That would mean they could choose one or the other. It says and, which means they commit to be together through both the light and dark side of whatever will come

Love wraps itself around a relationship and creates a space in which two people live. In that sense love is like gravity. It provides security, pleasure, freedom, comfort, strength, inspiration, openness, protection, care, joy, definition—in other words, it shapes and contains, responds to and directs, encourages and prods, two people and the relationship they form

Through love we bestow value on each other. Through love we challenge each other when we see something in the relationship that is less than it could be. Through love we imagine the future and create a vision that guides how we live day to day. Sometimes love is logical, reasonable, down-to-earth, and practical. At other times it is wild, flooded with enthusiasm and anticipation.

Sometimes we sense the eternal. Then again love helps us appreciate the magic in the mundane

Love is at the basis of the attraction two people feel toward one another, fueling their desire to feel the oneness that lays quietly beneath the diversity we see and feel. Sometimes love whispers. Sometimes it roars. Sometimes it is a gentle nudge. Sometimes it's like a swift wind that wraps around us so that we can hardly stand in its presence

During the years we've been together, we've never doubted the love we feel for one another and for the relationship we are co-creating. There have been some very tough times. Enduring them, love brought us closer together. There have been times that felt light and free, like stones skipping across a smooth lake. Enjoying them, love was the sparkle that shone in so many thousand winks from the tips of the waves

There have been times when we've sat quietly, still, listening. Love was there in the silence, like a trusted ally who is there without any need to call attention to himself

Truly, love is like gravity, holding everything together.

It is easier to fight for one's principles than to live up to them.

--Alfred Adler

35. THE MAGIC OF DIFFERENCE

In the past couples were more likely to live in the same town, even the same house, for much of their marriage. He usually stayed at the same job throughout, and she coordinated their social schedule with a group of family and friends that seldom varied. Their priorities were security and predictability

Now, as people change jobs and dwelling places almost as readily as kids outgrow their clothes, marriages must be based on far more than the old intimacy, which was largely dictated by sex-role stereotypes

In the new intimacy, the differences between the two unique individuals are the substance of their growing romance and intimacy. Like bread and jam, the magic happens when you put them together, yet neither one loses their special taste and texture

When we met, Jim was super laid-back, read and wrote poetry, loved dogs, and hated his job as an investment banker. Judith was compulsive and controlled, loved to travel, and was a successful psychologist of 10 years with a thriving private practice. She also felt

81

cloistered, seldom getting out of her office into the larger world

There were many, many differences between us that had to be discussed, navigated, and resolved. Sometimes heated fights erupted— we can each be pretty combustible! Yet in the process we were both improved by the influence of the other. Jim was the delicious jam to Judith's great homemade bread

Now Jim is far more organized, professionally visionary, and loves all the ways he gets to express himself through our work. Judith is much more easy going, loves to improvise on the radio, and is dedicated to teaching people to rejoice in their differences. Together we get to be out in the world with new people all the time

We have fertilized each other's worlds with our differences—and that is what the new intimacy does. It creates a loving, romantic miracle between two previously separate individuals

It truly is a miracle and it can be yours—whether with your lover, your children, or your friends. Anyone!

Free Questionnaire
Judith & Jim Invite You..
To Now Learn More About
Your Own Unconscious Loyalties...
You Can Begin Your Journey to Freedom
By Answering The Special FREE-To-Yo
"Unlock Your Full Potential Questionnaire
That Judith & Jim Have Created For You..
Just go to:
http://UnlockYourFullPotential.com/Questionnaire

Note: Before you Click "Submit" be sure to enter your Primary Email Address. And then put our email address in your email address book so you are sure not to miss a thing

judithandijm@judithandjim.co

To Helping You Unlock Your Full Potential!

Judith Sherven and James Sniechowski

Acknowledgement

First, we want to acknowledge all of Whitney Houston's fans around the world whose lives were touched, if not changed, by her magical gifts.

Second, we want to thank everyone who encouraged us to write this book, to use Whitney's story as an example of what happens to millions of people every day as they lose their lives to unconscious loyalties they have no awareness about.

And we are indebted to everyone who read a variety of drafts of this book, giving us their input and support: Signe Dayhoff, Tonja Johnson, Kashonia Carnegie, Art Klein, Tom Albertsson, Baeth Davis, Jim Duffie, Sarah Hopkins, Kelly Cline, Melody Starr, Louise LeBrun, Pam Brown, Maurice Dobbs, Kellie Frazier, Wendy Lucas, Jeremy Palmer, Alex Giorgio, Marie Berry, and Rex and Jill Wisehart.

Thank you to Miriam Pace for her artistic and technical talents in getting this book set up and published through JayEss Publishing, ready for our readers in eBook, Audio book, Kindle and Nook, and Paperback.

And finally, we want to thank everyone who, over the years, has helped us define and expand our "Overcoming The Fear of Being Fabulous" work, supporting us in creating and amplifying the variety of specifics that ground and make vivid the process of unconscious holdbacks.

About Judith & Jim

As a husband and wife psychology team and best-selling authors Judith Sherven, PhD and Jim Sniechowski, PhD—best known as Judith & Jim—have spent nearly 50 years combined specializing in helping people—from top international executives and world famous movie stars, to couples, singles, and individuals---confront, understand, and release unconscious prohibitions against success that can show up no matter what levels of success people have already achieved.

Famous for their ability to dig deep into the heart of what holds people back while providing the recipe for permanent release from that internal prison, they currently specialize in executive coaching.

Their "Overcoming The Fear Of Being Fabulous" 12-CD program enables users to shatter the blindness that has been holding them back, guiding them through the necessary steps to release the hold backs and roadblocks to successful living and loving.

Their goal is to have the power of Unconscious Loyalty, The Love Grip, Allegiances and Forbiddances deeply understood and used worldwide by therapists, coaches, counselors, pastoral counselors, teachers and school counselors, prison personnel, athletic coaches, medical professionals, child care professionals, and, of course, parents and grandparents.

As guest experts they've been on over 2700 television and radio shows including Oprah, The View, 48 Hours,

Judith Sherven and James Sniechowski

MSNBC, CNN, and Canada AM.

They've been interviewed or published by hundreds of major publications including the Los Angeles Times, Chicago Tribune, USA Today, Boston Globe, Wall Street Journal, London Sunday Times. U.S. News and World Report, Newsday, San Francisco Chronicle, Washington Post, Miami Herald, The San Juan Star (Puerto Rico), Cosmo, Glamour, Playboy, Barrister, Newsweek, Woman's Day, Utne Reader, Men's Health, Best Life, Reason, Bridal Guide, Recovery Times (London), Redbook, Essence, Vogue, Gioia (Italy), Mentor Magazine (Australia), Penthouse (Australia), Family Circle, Parents, Brides, and Today's Black Woman.

Meeting on a blind date March 7, 1987, Judith & Jim married 13 months later.

Other Books by Judith & Jim

The New Intimacy: Discovering The Magic At The Heart of Your Differences
Kindle: http://tinyurl.com/k9k7f
Paperback: https://www.createspace.com/3538798

Opening to Love 365 Days a Year
http://tinyurl.com/cfbrz
Be Loved for Who You Really Are,
http://tinyurl.com/dlmfc

The Smart Couple's Guide to the Wedding of Your Dreams: Planning Together for Less Stress and More Joy
http://www.tinyurl.com/c8sd8
The Heart of Marketing: Love Your Customers and They Will Love You Back
http://tinyurl.com/theheartofmrktg

Contact Judith & Jim

Whether for Media Interviews, Speaking Engagements, or Expert Commentary please contact Judith & Jim through:

Email:

JudithandJim@JudithandJim.com (Jim)

Judith@JudithandJim.com (Judith)

Tonja@judithandjim.com (Tonja – Customer Care

Telephone:

877-810-765

Skype:

judithsherven

Website:

http://WhatReallyKilledWhitneyHouston.com

http://OvercomingTheFearOfBeingFabulous.com

http://JudithandJim.com

www.ingramcontent.com/pod-product-compliance
Lightning Source LLC
Chambersburg PA
CBHW060514280326
41933CB00014B/2958